AN APPLETREE DELUXE EDITION

TREES & SHRUBS

IRELAND'S FLORA AND FAUNA

A COMPACT ILLUSTRATED GUIDE SHOWING
TREES & SHRUBS FROM ACROSS IRELAND AS AN
AID TO IDENTIFICATION

PETER WYSE-JACKSON

AN APPLETREE DELUXE EDITION

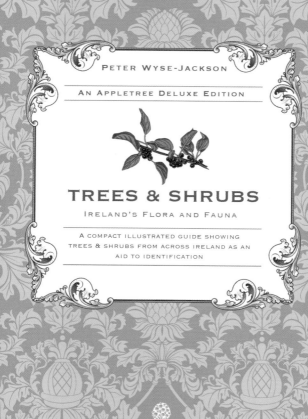

TREES & SHRUBS

IRELAND'S FLORA AND FAUNA

A COMPACT ILLUSTRATED GUIDE SHOWING
TREES & SHRUBS FROM ACROSS IRELAND AS AN
AID TO IDENTIFICATION

Appletree Press

First published in 2007 by
Appletree Press Ltd
The Old Potato Station
14 Howard Street South
Belfast
BT7 1AP

Tel: +44 (0) 28 90 24 30 74
Fax: +44 (0) 28 90 24 67 56
E-mail: reception@appletree.ie
Web Site: www.appletree.ie

First published in 1994 as *Irish Trees and Shrubs* by Appletree Press Ltd

A catalogue record for this book is available from the British Library.

TREES & SHRUBS – IRELAND'S FLORA & FAUNA

ISBN: 978 1 84758 054 2

Desk Editor: Jean Brown
Editor: Jim Black
Designer: Stuart Wilkinson
Production Manager: Paul McAvoy

9 8 7 6 5 4 3 2 1

AP3492

CONTENTS

CONTENTS

INTRODUCTION

This guide to Ireland's trees and shrubs describes and illustrates sixty-four of the common species of the countryside, as well as providing some hints to identifying a further thirty or forty other closely related species which are rarer. This book includes plants that are found naturally in Ireland (called natives) as well as many that have been introduced from other countries that have sometimes gone wild. The species are arranged in families, placed in botanical order, next to their closest relatives. The most primitive families come first and the most advanced families, in evolutionary terms come last. English, Irish and scientific (Latin) names are given for each species where possible. Unfortunately, some of the rarest species have neither Irish names nor commonly used English names.

The number of technical terms used in the book has been kept to a minimum but a short glossary is also given. A short list of other more comprehensive books on trees and shrubs relevant to Ireland is given for readers who wish to learn more about Irish flora. Most of the flowering times are as given by D. A. Webb in *An Irish Flora*.

Acknowledgements: I am grateful to my family for all their help, especially my wife, Diane, and my brothers John and Michael for reading the text and for their useful suggestions.

Peter S. Wyse Jackson

Noble Fir
Abies procera
Giúis

Noble Fir

This handsome tree grows up to about 50 metres (165 feet) in Ireland and is used in forestry in western areas where it has proved to be quite resistant to strong winds and harsh weather. It is also widely planted in parks and large gardens. It is originally native to the US in Oregon and Washington.

The Noble Fir has a pyramidal shape, with smooth bark when young which becomes rough and fissured when mature, rather variable in colour from pale grey to purplish. Its needles are 1.5 to 3.5 cm long, about 1.5 mm wide, bluish grey in colour and very densely arranged at the top and sides of the shoots. When they drop they leave a flat circular scar on the smooth twigs. The Noble fir has large erect cones up to 30 cm and 9 cm across, purplish brown when mature. This species makes an attractive Christmas tree and holds onto its needles even when dead, unlike those of the more frequently used *Picea*. Evergreen; flowers in May.

Sitka Spruce
Picea sitchensis
Sprús sitceach

Sitka Spruce

The Sitka spruce is the most popular and widely planted forestry tree in Ireland. It is native to the western seaboard of North America from Alaska to California. It grows up to 60 metres (200 feet) tall, and is a conical tree with grey bark peeling in small scales. Its branches are stiff and slightly upturned, except the side shoots which droop somewhat. Its needles are 15 to 30 mm long, have a slate-grey or bluish tint, are striped underneath with two white bands and end with a sharp point. When they drop off they leave a small raised peg behind, an easy way to recognise a *Picea*. *Picea* has pegs, in *Abies* they are absent. Its cones are 6 to 10 cm long, pendulous, pale brown in colour, with thin papery scales which have crinkly toothed edges – *Abies* has ascending cones.

Sitka spruce grows well in wet, peaty soils and in high rainfall areas. Its growth can be very rapid – more than one metre (3.3 feet) per annum. Its timber is used for telegraph poles, fencing, chipboard and hardboard manufacture and in house building. It is the major tree used for cellulose in paper milling. Evergreen; flowers in May.

European Larch
Larix decidua
Learóg

European Larch

This deciduous conifer native to the Alps is quite widely planted in Ireland for forestry, in parks and large gardens, on roadsides and in shelter belts. It is a tall, conical and fast-growing tree up to 35 metres (115 feet). Its needles are mainly in spiral clusters on short woody spurs off the branches. The needles are soft, 12 to 30 mm long, pale green and turning yellowish in autumn before falling. The tips of the shoots hang down and give the tree a vaguely weeping look. The male cones begin whitish but become yellow as they shed their pollen. Female cones are usually rosy-red when young and 20 to 40 mm long by 20 to 30 mm wide when ripe. Many trees retain the old dead cones on their branches for several years.

Another closely related species widely planted is the Japanese larch, *Larix kaempferi*, and there is also an intermediate hybrid between the two, *Larix x eurolepis*. The Japanese larch is much broader leaved than the European larch and a darker grey-green, not weeping. Its smaller cones have the upper edge of the cone-scales rolled back, and the whole tree is more densely branched. Larch timber is strong and one of the most durable conifer woods. It is widely used for fences, gates, estate repair work and for fishing boats. Deciduous; flowers from March to April.

Scots Pine
Pinus sylvestris
Péine albanach

Scots Pine

The Scots pine is pyramidal when young but becomes a fine and tall flat-topped tree when mature. Its fissured and flaking chocolate-reddish bark is an easily spotted characteristic of the species even at some distance. Its needles are in pairs, grey-green in colour and stiffly twisted, 4 to 8 cm long. Its male cones are very small and massed together in clusters at the start of the new year's growth. The female cones are also small, 3 to 4 mm long only, dark red, in groups of two to five at the ends of stronger shoots. The female cones take two seasons to mature and eventually reach a length of 3 to 7 cm. When the cones dry out in drier spells the seeds are shed.

The Scots pine was common in Ireland 7,000 to 9,000 years ago when the climate was drier. It died out in about AD 300 when the Atlantic climatic influences made Ireland a wetter and warmer place. It was reintroduced in about 1700 and is now commonly planted and well established in most counties. The nearest native stands of the Scots pine are in the Highlands of Scotland. In many Irish bogs remnant stumps of large pine forests long submerged have been revealed where the peat has been cut away. Scots pine also occurs in Europe eastwards to Siberia. Its timber was much used for railway sleepers and telegraph poles. Evergreen; flowers from May to June.

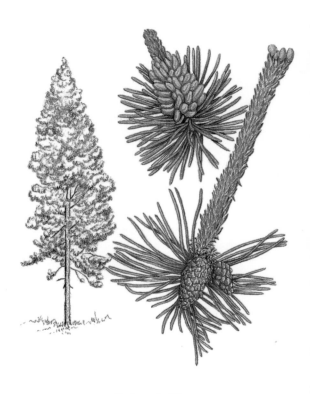

Lodgepole Pine
Pinus contorta
Péine contórtach

Lodgepole Pine

The lodgepole pine is common in commercial forestry in Ireland and can attain a height of more than 25 metres (80 feet) as a tall and rather narrow tree. It has a fissured and reddish bark often patterned with small, squarish plates. Its needles are in pairs, somewhat twisted, arranged very densely, especially on the younger vigorous shoots, which vary in colour from deep green to yellowish green, and in length from 4 to 7 cm. The ripe female cones are 2 to 6 cm long and occur in whorls of two to five, and are oval to conical in shape.

Lodgepole pine is not particularly well suited to limestone soils, but has been used as an effective pioneer tree for bogs, coastal sands and dry sandy soils. It is native to western North America from Alaska to California and into the Rocky Mountains. Although the species varies considerably throughout its natural range, its coastal form is the variety generally planted in Ireland. Evergreen; flowers from May to June.

Monterey Pine
Pinus radiata
Péine

Monterey Pine

The Monterey pine is native only to a few small areas of California. In Ireland there are probably many times the number of trees than survive in their natural habitat. It is a rapidly growing tree which reaches up to 35 metres (115 feet) tall in the British Isles and so is quite commonly planted for forestry and in parks. Growth rates of up to 2.5 metres (8 feet) per annum have been recorded. However, it is not completely hardy and can be damaged by hard frosts.

It has grey-brown and deeply fissured bark and a conical shape to its crown. Its branches are at first drooping but turn upwards at their ends as they elongate. The bright green needles are in threes, very slender, straight and reach 10 cm or more in length. The male cones are small and bright yellow in spring. The female cones vary in size, 7 to 20 cm in length and 6 to 10 cm across, light glossy reddish brown in colour, oval and very asymmetrical at the base. The cones tend to be retained on the branches long after they have ripened and shed their seeds.

A wide range of other fine species are cultivated in Ireland, especially in large gardens, parks and demesnes. These are mainly from Europe, North America and Asia, although some species occur native to Central and South America. Worldwide, over ninety species of pine are known. Evergreen; flowers in April.

Juniper
Juniperus communis
Aiteal

Juniper

The juniper can be either an upright or a prostrate bushy shrub. It has red-brown flaking bark and short, stiff and prickly needle-like leaves, 0.5 to 2 cm long, blue-green in colour, arranged in a whorl of three around the shoot. Male and female flowers occur in cones but grow on separate trees. The male cones are small and rather inconspicuous. The female cones also begin very small but swell to form green berry-like fruits that turn blue-black on ripening, eventually reaching a size of 6 to 9 mm long.

Two subspecies of the juniper occur in Ireland. Subsp. *communis* can be either upright or prostrate, with sharply pointed leaves, growing on limestone soils. Subsp. *alpina* is always prostrate and has broader incurved, blunter leaves and grows mainly on acid soils. It is commonest in Connemara. Although a wide range of exotic junipers are grown in gardens, in the wild it is not common except in rocky places, on mountains and lake shores in the west and north-west of Ireland, especially in Kerry, Clare, Donegal and Connemara.

A native of Ireland, in the past its foliage was used for kindling. It has a fragrant smell when burnt. Juniper oil is an important constituent of gin and a peppery spice may be obtained from its seeds. Evergreen; flowers in May.

Yew
Taxus baccata
iúr

Yew

Almost every old churchyard in Ireland has a yew tree. Even in pre-Christian Ireland the yew was associated with religious sites. Yew wood has long been prized for its durability and is decorative for cabinet-making. The oldest human tool ever found in Europe is a spear made of yew wood lodged in the ribs of a straight-tusked palaeolithic elephant in Lower Saxony. The best bows were also made of yew wood.

Yew grows to be a large spreading tree or shrub up to 25 metres (80 feet) tall with reddish peeling or flaking bark. Its leaves are dark green on top with two pale stripes underneath. They are flat, long and narrow, 10 to 40 mm in length, and although they are attached almost spirally to their shoots they appear to be in a row on each side of the shoot. Yew fruits consist of a seed about 6 mm in length surrounded by a scarlet cup-shaped fleshy coat called an aril. Although the seeds themselves are known to be poisonous, the aril is not.

A native of Ireland, the yew is rare in the wild and occurs mainly in woods and rocky places and cliffs in the west (especially the Burren and Kerry) and in the north. Evergreen; flowers in March.

London Plane
Platanus x hebrida
Plána Londan

London Plane

The London plane is a frequent street tree in Ireland. It is easily recognised by its peeling bark which is ideal for the city environment. By the time the bark is dirty and grimy with pollution it is dropped as large flakes like peeling scabs. It is also easy to prune without killing the tree, which then sprouts freely again.

Its leaves are like those of the maple, similar to the sycamore but spikier. It can also be distinguished from maples by its alternate leaves and by its enlarged leaf-stalk bases. Maples have opposite leaves. Its flowers occur usually in two globular heads which hang on long stalks. The fruits develop in the winter and are spiky, globular and rather woody. Deciduous; flowers from June to July.

INTRODUCTION TO THE
ELM FAMILY

Elms have long been important street, timber and hedgerow trees. Today, their populations have been devastated by Dutch elm disease, which spread like wildfire through the countryside wiping out every mature tree in most districts. The disease is caused by a fungus and is spread from tree to tree by a beetle. The fungus blocks the sap vessels of the tree, first killing individual branches and then the whole tree.

Nowadays, most elms found are multi-stemmed scrubby trees that have arisen as suckers sprouted from the bases of diseased trees. The identification of elm species is not easy, even for experts. The identification of suckers can be almost impossible.

Elm flowers are small, in dense reddish-brown clusters and open before the leaves in spring. Their fruits are composed of a single seed, completely surrounded by a leafy green wing, with a deep notch at the top.

Irish Elm, Wych Elm • Ulmus glabra • *Leamhán sléibhe*

The wych elm is a large tree with spreading branches. It has been commonly planted in most areas but is rare as a native, except in remoter parts of the north-west and west where pockets of trees unaffected by disease still occur. Leaves are large (10 to 12 cm long), undivided and roughly toothed along their edge, broadly oval and pointed with very asymmetrical bases and rough upper surfaces. Deciduous; flowers from March to April.

English Elm
Ulmus procera
Leamhán gallda

English Elm

The English elm grows to be a tall, massive and very erect tree. It has leaves up to 8 cm long, smaller than the previous species, rough on their upper surface and longer leaf-stalks (4 to 6 mm) than the wych elm.

Ulmus minor (or *U. carpinifolia*), the small-leaved elm (Leamhán mion), is an introduction to Ireland. It is less frequently seen than the Irish species. It has leaf-stalks 6 to 12 mm long, hairless or nearly hairless twigs (the other species have hairy twigs) and smooth upper surfaces to its leaves.

The timber of the elm is one of the most prized. It is very resistant to splitting and therefore ideal for furniture (and coffins). It is slow to rot in water when kept wet and thus the first water pipes from the Middle Ages onwards were made from elm. Indeed, many of the fine and ancient elms in Dublin, now gone, were planted first for this purpose and only survived because lead pipes became popular instead, only to be killed by disease in more recent years. Deciduous; flowers from March to April.

Bog Myrtle
Myrica gale
Roideóg

Bog Myrtle

Bog myrtle is the most characteristic bushy species of Irish bogs and is also found on some lake shores. A native, it is common in most of the west although it becomes rarer towards the east. It is a small bushy species which obtained its name from the myrtle-like aroma given off by its shoots when crushed. It was formerly used as a source of candle wax which gave off a delicious perfume as it burned. As a rustic bedding in the Middle Ages, it was a useful species to keep away fleas and was used to flavour beer before hops became the norm. An old tradition in Ireland says that the bog myrtle was once a great tree but was condemned to the bogs as a scruffy little shrub because it had been used to make the cross for Christ's crucifixion.

It grows to a height of about 1 metre (3.3 feet), is deciduous and has hairless, long (6 cm) and narrow (2 cm), dark green, slightly glossy leaves. Its flowers are borne in catkins appearing in early spring before the leaves open. Male and female flowers occur on separate catkins; the male catkins are about 15 mm long and the female ones shorter, up to 6 mm. Deciduous; flowers from April to May.

Beech
Fagus sylvatica
Feá

Beech

Beech is not native in Ireland although magnificent native beech woods occur as close as south-east England. Nevertheless, pollen fossils of beech have been found near Gort, County Galway, dating from a warm period many thousands of years earlier, suggesting that it once was a native tree. Not being as frequent here, beech timber never gained the importance in Ireland that it had in England where it was widely used, especially for furniture.

Beech can grow to a height of up to 40 metres (130 feet) and has a characteristic smooth silvery grey bark. Its leaves are alternate, short-stalked, oval and entire, up to 10 cm long and 6 cm broad. They open a brilliant green with a fringe of silvery, silky hairs along their edges. In autumn they turn to attractive shades of yellow and red before falling. The long, narrow, brown, dormant winter buds are borne on fine slender twigs. The small male flowers appear in short catkins and the small female flowers in clusters of twos and threes. When ripe, the fruits occur as paired triangular-shaped nuts surrounded by a spiny husk or woody sheath that grows up from the base of the female flowers and then splits into four lobes to release the nuts. Deciduous; flowers from April to May.

Spanish Chestnut, Sweet Chestnut
Castanea sativa
Castán

Spanish Chestnut, Sweet Chestnut

The sweet chestnut is native to south-west Asia. It was probably introduced to southern Europe and North Africa by the Greeks and to the British Isles by the Romans as a food source. Its nuts are still widely collected and used in Europe; in Corsica they are a staple food. Their kernels are dried and ground into a flour. Sadly, in Ireland the nuts do not often reach a very worthwhile size. The nuts can be boiled or roasted. The sweet chestnut has been widely planted in Ireland, especially in large gardens, parks and estate woodlands. It occasionally seeds itself.

It can grow to be an enormous and ancient tree, up to 30 metres (100 feet) tall with a trunk of huge girth. Its bark is covered by deep and regular fissures which weave their way around the trunk in a spiral. Its large leaves (up to 20 cm long) are dark green and glossy, narrow (about 7 cm across), tongue-shaped with holly-like points at the end of each vein. When young the leaves have a yellow "fur" underneath which later disappears. In summer, the tree produces creamy white male and female flowers in long catkin-like spikes. When the fruits ripen they are globular and very spiky to touch and contain one, two or three brown nuts, pointed at one end. Deciduous; flowers from June to July.

Sessile Oak, Common Oak
Quercus petraea
Dair ghaelach

Sessile Oak, Common Oak

The native common oak, Q. *petraea*, covered the upland, western and northern parts of Ireland, even on the poorer soils. It was and is less common in the midlands and in lowland areas. The best remaining oak woods are those in Killarney, County Kerry.

It is a tree up to 40 metres (130 feet) tall with grey bark marked with narrow, shallow fissures. Its leaves are more or less oval but with five to nine deep rounded lobes on each side, about 12 cm long and 7 cm wide with a leaf-stalk of about 2.5 cm. Its leaves are quite leathery, glossy green above and have rather a pale grey-green and hairy underside. Its male flowers are in catkins 5 to 8 cm long while the female flowers are small and borne at the ends of the shoots. The acorns (fruits) are about 3 cm long and may or may not have very short stalks. Deciduous; flowers in May.

English Oak, Pedunculate Oak
Quercus robur
Dair ghallda

English Oak, Pedunculate Oak

A native of Ireland, the pedunculate oak, *Q. robur*, is found on the better Irish soils but only a few midland woods survive. It grows up to be a tall tree, ultimately somewhat taller than the common oak. It has pale grey bark marked with narrow vertical fissures. Its leaves are similar in shape to the sessile oak but are generally smaller (up to 10 cm long); furthermore, they lack a stalk, are hairless underneath and have two small upturned lobes, called auricles, at the leaf-base. The male flowers are in bunches of very slender catkins 2 to 5 cm long and the female flowers are small and at the ends of the shoots. The acorns have a long stalk usually between 4 and 8 cm long, a useful characteristic to distinguish them from *Q. petraea*. Deciduous; flowers in May.

INTRODUCTION TO THE
BIRCH FAMILY

There are two native birches in Ireland. Both are attractive, elegant and slender trees. They are "colonist" trees, being often amongst the first trees to become established in a new site. The two Irish species are not always easy to distinguish, even for an expert. They often cross to produce hybrids which may be intermediate in morphology between the two. Birch has had many uses in the past in Ireland. In prehistoric times the trees were laid down to make trackways through marshy ground and their bark used to waterproof floors. The timber is not much used now but can make attractive veneers and has been employed for cotton reels, herring barrels, plywood, clogs and even modern aeroplane propellers. Birch twigs are also flexible and strong, ideal for use in corporal punishment!

Silver Birch • Betula pendula • *Beith gheal*

The silver birch is a tall, slender and attractive tree up to 30 metres (100 feet) with silvery white peeling bark. Its delicate branches are gently drooping at their tips. Young shoots are hairless and covered with slightly raised pale green resin-filled glands. The leaves are 2.5 to 7 cm long, oval to somewhat triangular in shape with long points and edged with sharp double teeth. The catkins appear at the same time as the leaves. The male catkins are 30 to 60 mm long and occur at the ends of the branches while the female ones are 15 to 35 mm and are produced along the shoots.

Widely planted in gardens, hedges and estate woods, the silver birch is also used as a street tree in Ireland. It appears as a rare native tree in parts of the midlands and south, beside lakes, in scrubby woods, bogs and on sandy soils, and occurs throughout Europe except in the drier and warmer parts of the south. Deciduous; flowers from April to May.

41

Downy Birch
Betula pubescens
Beith chlúmhach

Downy Birch

This is a slender small tree or shrub up to about 25 metres (80 feet). It has brown, grey or rarely off-white peeling bark and spreading branches which do not droop at their tips. Young shoots are usually covered in soft down and are without resin glands, although, in the west, some trees can be found which are more or less hairless and which have brown resin glands and so may seem similar to the silver birch. Its leaves are up to 55 mm long, oval to triangular but more rounded than the previous species and with a shorter point. Their edges have irregular teeth. The catkins are similar to those of the silver birch but have scales that are spreading or curved upwards. Both species have seeds with broad membrane-like wings. Deciduous; flowers from April to May.

Common Adler
Alnus glutinosa
Fearnóg

Common Adler

The common alder is a smallish, often rather inconspicuous and overlooked tree. It is very widespread in Europe, Asia and North Africa and common throughout Ireland in damp and moist habitats. It often grows on stream, river and lake shores and banks, thriving in boggy soils and in moist woodlands.

As a timber tree it is little used now. In Britain it was used to make clogs as its timber is a poor conductor of heat. Its wood is useful and long-lasting in a moist situation; indeed much of the city of Venice rests on alder piles.

Its leaves are dark green, round or broadly oval with bluntly toothed edges, 4 to 7 cm across. Separate male and female catkins are produced in early spring. The long male catkins are dark purple in colour and drooping in clusters generally of three to five. The female cones open later and are short and ovoid, dark brown and woody when ripe. These female catkins persist on the tree after the leaves have dropped, which themselves can stay on the tree until winter. The alder is not a very remarkable tree and in Ireland was often regarded as unlucky. Nevertheless, it has a quiet, self-assured dignity and grows well even in the most apparently unfavourable situations.

A close relative, although not a native, the grey alder, *Alnus incana* (Fearnóg liath), is occasionally planted and gone wild in a few areas. It has toothed and pointed leaves that are paler underneath than those of *A. glutinosa*. Deciduous; flowers in March.

Hornbeam
Carpinus betulus
Crann sleamhain

Hornbeam

The hornbeam is native to the south-eastern counties of Britain but has been widely planted in Ireland, especially in estate woodlands. It is a popular species for high-class hedges. In a few areas it has seeded itself in the wild. It gains its name from its timber which is as hard as horn and was formerly used for many of the toughest tasks for which wood was required, such as cogs, pulleys and wood screws, skittles, mallets and brush backs. It is sometimes called "iron-wood". In England, some ancient hornbeam coppice woodlands still survive but in Ireland its role has probably been purely an ornamental one.

Hornbeam most frequently grows as a shrub, but when it becomes a tree it has a distinctive fluted trunk and smooth grey bark. Its leaves are oval in shape, toothed and pointed about 8 cms long by 5 cm broad, and more or less hairless. Flowers occur in catkins: the male catkins are 3 cm long and the female catkins up to 7 cm long with conspicuous long green bracts (which turn brown before falling) at the base of which are the small nuts. Deciduous; flowers from April to May.

Hazel
Corylus avellana
Coll

Hazel

One of the most widespread woodland plants in Ireland is the hazel. It is typically a bushy multi-stemmed shrub between 1 to 6 metres (3 to 20 feet) tall in oak and ash woods but may rarely become a small tree. It was widely used for coppice to provide slender sticks for many purposes: fences, fuel, hurdles, hoops for barrels (before these were replaced by metal bands). Their nuts are excellent to eat, although there is no commercial production of them in Ireland that I know of. The hazel has always been a special tree in Ireland, used to ward off evil spirits and fairies. A hazelnut carried in the pocket was said to keep away lumbago and rheumatism.

Hazel leaves are alternately arranged, rather wrinkled, about 10 cm long, oval to almost round with a pointed tip and jaggedly double-toothed edge, light green and softly hairy. The twigs are also hairy and covered with reddish, slightly sticky (glandular) hairs. Male catkins are about 8 cm long, bright yellow and hanging down like lambs' tails but in clusters of up to four. The female catkins are much smaller, like tiny buds 5 mm long from which the bright red styles protrude. The fruits ripen as brown hard-shelled nuts about 1.5 cm long contained with a shaggy leaf-like cup.

A native of Ireland, hazel occurs commonly in hedgerows and woodlands and sometimes as dense thickets where it can be the dominant species, such as in the hazel scrubs of the Burren in County Clare. Deciduous; flowers from February to March.

White Poplar
Populus alba
Poibleog

White Poplar

The white poplar is a distinctive, attractive and strong-growing spreading tree usually 15 to 20 metres (50 to 65 feet) and rarely up to 40 metres (130 feet). It prefers moist soft ground but often leans as a result. Numerous suckers usually grow around well-established trees which can become quite a nuisance for gardeners. It is native to central and south-east Europe and extends eastwards to central Asia.

It has grey or blackish bark, often fissured lower down and smooth further up the trunk. Its young shoots and twigs are densely covered in white hairs. The leaves of the white poplar are very distinctive and striking even from a distance: shaped like maple leaves, 3 to 10 centimetres long and wide, dark green on top and densely covered with pure white hairs underneath. Most if not all the Irish trees are female. Their catkins are 3 to 5 cm long, brown and hairy, with greenish stigmas. Deciduous; flowers from February to March.

Aspen
Populus tremula
Crann creathach

Aspen

On a breezy day the aspen is an easy tree to identify. Its leaf-stalks are flattened in an unusual way, from side to side, allowing the leaves to "shake like an aspen" and to rustle noisily in the wind. The aspen can grow to be a tree of up to 20 metres (65 feet) tall with smooth grey bark, but it often occurs as a suckering shrub in hedgerows. A native of Ireland, it is commonest in the west and north of the country in hedgerows and rocky and wild areas, generally on the poorest soils. It is much less frequent in the east and south and where it occurs it has usually been planted.

Its twigs are dull greyish brown and more or less hairless. The leaves are alternate, 1.5 to 8 cm long and 3 to 5 cm across, ranging from broadly oval to almost circular, roughly and irregularly toothed, quite pale green in colour and lighter underneath. The leaves on young suckers may vary more in shape and tend to be hairy and more regularly toothed. Catkins are 5 to 8 cm long and male and female ones occur on separate trees. The male catkins have reddish purple anthers and the female catkins have pink stigmas. The timber of the aspen is used for making matches and wooden matchboxes as it is light and easy to work.

Populus x canescens, the grey poplar *(Poibleog lia)*, is a hybrid between the white poplar, *P. alba*, and the aspen. It is quite commonly planted and well established in many sites, especially in woods and hedges. It differs from the aspen by having more deeply divided leaves and lots of grey hairs on the leaf undersides. It spreads easily by suckers. Deciduous; flowers from February to March.

Black Poplar
Populus nigra
Poibleog dhubh

54

Black Poplar

The black poplar may be a native Irish tree, although a rare one. It has been found especially in the midlands, predominantly in hedgerows in wet farmland near deep water-filled ditches, particularly along the River Shannon. It is a tall tree growing up to 35 metres (115 feet) with rough fissured dark grey bark. Its twigs are a shiny orange-brown, smooth and more or less hairless. The leaves are triangular oval, 5 to 10 cm long with toothed edges, bright glossy green on top and paler beneath. The leaf-stalks are flattened from side to side, like those of the aspen but less markedly so. Male and female flowers (in catkins) occur on separate trees. The male catkins have distinctive crimson anthers and the female catkins have green stigmas. The catkins open 3 to 5 cm long and gradually elongate as they ripen.

The most familiar and commonly planted variety in Ireland is the Lombardy poplar, *P. nigra var. italica*. It is tall, upright and narrow. Lombardy poplars are often planted in long avenues, a use for which they are particularly badly suited as they are fragile and mature quickly but then may become dangerous. Deciduous; flowers from March to April.

INTRODUCTION TO THE
WILLOW FAMILY

There are more than a dozen willows found in the wild in Ireland, although not all are natives. They vary from small shrubs to several large trees. Most thrive in the wettest soils, in bogs, ditches and river banks but many of the common species will grow almost anywhere and are easy to cultivate, rooting easily from cuttings, no matter which way up they are planted. All willows have catkins with male or female flowers without petals or sepals. Another characteristic they share is the single scale that surrounds each bud, most noticeable in winter.

The identification of different willow species is not easy, especially as most cross freely with each other to form hybrids which may be intermediate between their parents in morphology. Hybrids between *Salix cinerea*, *S. aurita* and *S. caprea* are very common.

Crack Willow, Withy • Salix fragilis • *Saileach bhriosc*

Introduced into Ireland, this is a very fast-growing tree that can grow to a height of 25 metres (80 feet). It gains its name by having brittle twigs and branches that can easily be broken off with a "crack". Its twigs are generally yellow-brown in colour. When planted at the water's edge, a tangled mass of conspicuous red vein-like roots often grows into the water. It is often pollarded to sprout a mass of slender shoots ideal for basketmaking. It is commonly planted and occurs on river and stream banks, ditches and many wet habitats on marshy soils.

Its leaves are about five times as long as broad, lanceolate, with a finely toothed edge, often rather blue-green underneath usually 7 to 10 cm long, having silky hairs when young and then becoming hairless. Its catkins are long and drooping and appear at much the same time as the leaves. The male catkins are 2.5 to 6 cm long and the females 3 to 7 cm. Its stipules are long and narrow. Deciduous; flowers from April to May.

White Willow
Salix alba
Saileach bhán

White Willow

The white willow is a beautiful pyramid-shaped tree up to 25 metres (80 feet) tall with grey-green foliage. It is similar to the withy except that it has branches that are more erect, and also lacks the fragile twigs and shorter, less drooping catkins. This species is also often pollarded. A distinct variety, *var. caerulea*, is the cricket bat willow with more blue-green coloured leaves and upright branches, and another, var. vitellina, is highly decorative with bright yellow or orange twigs. White willow bark was widely used for tanning leather.

The leaves of the white willow are lanceolate, narrower than those of the crack willow, about ten times as long as broad, 5 to 10 cm long, and are covered with white silky hairs on both the upper and lower surfaces. An introduced species, this tree is common throughout Ireland in hedges, river and stream banks and in a wide range of wet soil habitats. Deciduous; flowers from April to May.

Osier
Salix viminalis
Saileánach

Osier

This very vigorous shrub or tree, 3 to 6 metres (10 to 20 feet) tall, is often pollarded and cropped to give a head of long, straight flexible twigs used for basketmaking. Introduced to Ireland, it is widely planted and many of the mature trees seen are a relict of cultivation. Basketmaking was one of the most widespread rural crafts and Connemara and Lough Neagh were famed for the quality of their baskets.

Its leaves are long, up to 20 cm in length, eight to twenty times as long as broad, hairless above but covered with silvery, silky hairs beneath. Leaf edges are enrolled and slightly wavy. Its twigs are often yellowish brown. Catkins are 12 to 30 mm long, erect, appearing before the leaves. Stipules are very narrow.

The osier is common in all parts of Ireland. It is a conspicuous tree, occurring on riversides, banks and ditches. Deciduous; flowers from April to May.

Goat Willow • Salix caprea • *Sailchearnach*

This is a large shrub or small tree growing up to 10 metres (32 feet) tall, and occasionally more. Its leaves are dark green, hairless and relatively smooth above but wrinkled and covered with grey down underneath, oval to oblong or almost round, shortly pointed, up to 13 cm long, and about one and a half times as long as broad. Stipules are small and ear-shaped. Its catkins are15 to 25 mm long and appear before the leaves. It is one of the most easily recognised willows in Ireland with its large and broad leaves.

This species was cut on Palm Sunday in Ireland, and a staff of this willow carried on a journey was said to be lucky. It is native and a common species through the country, occurring on damp and rough ground, in woods and hedges, and not only in wet habitats. Deciduous; flowers from March to April.

Eared Willow • Salix aurita • *Crann sníofa*

The eared willow is a shrub from 1 to 3 metres (3–10 feet) in height with many spreading branches. Its leaves are dull grey-green in colour and very wrinkled on their upper surface, grey and hairy underneath, one and a half to three times as long as broad, 2 to 3 cm long, and vary in shape from oblong to oval. Catkins are ovoid in shape, erect, 2 to 3 cm long, appearing before the leaves. Stipules are large, leafy and toothed.

A native of Ireland, this is a common shrub, especially of mountain and moorland, occurring on stream banks, field margins and by ditches and in damp scrubby woods. Deciduous; flowers from March to April.

Sally, Rusty Willow
Salix cinerea
Saileach rua

Sally, Rusty Willow

The sally is a robust shrub or small tree up to 10 metres (32 feet) tall. Its twigs are downy when young and become hairless as they mature. The leaves are rather variable in shape, oval to lanceolate, two to three and a half times as long as broad, slightly downy on top (but not wrinkled like the eared willow), blue-green below with variously coloured hairs. Leaf edges are inrolled and toothed. Ear-shaped stipules are usually present but are quite small. Catkins are 20 to 30 mm long and appear before the leaves.

A native to Ireland, two subspecies of this occur: subsp. *oleifolia*, the rusty willow, and subsp. *cinerea*, the grey willow. However, they are difficult to distinguish, though the former tends to have rusty red hairs under the leaves while the latter has grey hairs.

This is probably the commonest Irish willow, occurring in hedges, field margins, by ditches, streamside and river banks and in scrubby woodlands. Deciduous; flowers from March to April.

Rhododendron
Rhododendron ponticum
Ródaideandrón, Róslabhras

Rhododendron

A large range of rhododendron species and hybrids are grown in Irish gardens. They grow best in acid (lime-free) soils and occur in a wide range of colours.

Most garden rhododendrons are native to the Himalayas. However, *R. ponticum* comes from Turkey and from a small area in Spain. During at least one warm period in the Ice Age, *R. ponticum* was found naturally in Ireland, but when the ice returned the species was pushed south and left to survive only in these two widely separated localities. It returned during the 19th century when it was planted in woodland demesnes to provide cover for pheasants. It certainly liked Ireland's woodlands and wet boggy mountainsides and so quickly spread by seed and vegetatively to colonise many wild habitats that it is now regarded as a beautiful but dangerous weed.

R. ponticum can grow to 3 metres (10 feet) tall and is an evergreen shrub. Its leaves are dark green, oblong and about 12 by 6 cm in size. The numerous large (about 5 cm across) purple flowers are clustered together in heads at the ends of the shoots. Evergreen; flowers from May to June.

Strawberry Tree

The strawberry tree is a large shrub or medium-sized evergreen tree native to the Mediterranean coast of Europe, Brittany and Ireland. It is found rarely in Cork and Kerry and by Lough Gill in Sligo, but its Irish stronghold is around Killarney in County Kerry.

It is generally found on dry soil between rocks, in woodland margins and on islands and lake shores where most specimens are probably extremely ancient. It is also a popular garden plant usually grown as a bushy shrub. It has alternate oval leaves which are slightly toothed, 5 to 8 cm long, leathery and hairless. When mature, the tree has a reddish bark that is papery and flakey. Its flowers are white and like those of lily-of-the-valley, sometimes tinged with green or pink, in drooping clusters. These are followed by fruits that are a rich red colour, rough-skinned and round. They look very like strawberries, attractive looking and edible when ripe. However, the species name "*unedo*" implies that eating one fruit would be more than enough. Fruit and flower clusters hang on the tree together in early winter, as the previous year's fruit matures just as the present year's flowers bloom.

During the Middle Ages in Ireland it is said to have been a popular tree with charcoal burners and may have been exterminated from many areas with woodland clearance. The Irish name, *Caithne*, occurs occasionally, especially in the west.

The strawberry tree is one of Ireland's few native evergreens and is a most interesting plant. It is not native to Britain. The English botanist, John Parkinson, referred to it in his Theatrum Botanicum, published in 1640, reporting it remarkable that this tree grew in Ireland "of its own accord". Thomas Molyneux recorded in 1696, presumably with displeasure, that these

68

Strawberry Tree • Arbutus unedo • *Caithne*

trees, which did not grow in any "neighbouring kingdoms", were being cut up for fuel. There is one theory that the strawberry tree was first brought to Ireland from southern Europe by early monks, but this is thought to be unlikely. The tree is referred to in Brehon laws of the 8th century together with elder, blackthorn and some others.

The strawberry tree is more interesting than beautiful. It grows taller in Ireland than it does on the continent, and looks straggly and awkward out of the fruiting season, though the reddish bark is handsome. It is cultivated in large gardens for its striking fruit, and looks decorative at Christmas time if surrounded by more compact shrubs. There is a bushier variety "Croomei", with deep pink flowers. Evergreen; flowers from September to October.

Escallonia
Escallonia rubra var. macrantha

Escallonia

This common evergreen shrub is often grown as a hedge. It can reach a height of more than 3 metres (10 feet) but never becomes a tree. Native to Chile, it was introduced to the British Isles in 1846. It is quite tolerant of salt and is therefore frequent in mild coastal areas.

Its leaves are alternate, oval in shape, glossy green on top and sticky with tiny glands underneath. The leaves have toothed edges and are about 8 cm long and 5 cm broad. The flowers occur throughout the summer and have five rosy red petals about 1.5 cm long and broad, arranged in long (about 10 cm) heads at the ends of the branches.

There are three other hedge plants common in Ireland that might be confused with this and are worthy of note. Privet, *Ligustrum ovalifolium* is the first. "Hedge", *Lonicera nitida*, from China, with small roundish dark green leaves about 1 cm long, is a rather dull shrub but makes a useful and neat hedge. Another, *Griselinia littoralis*, is a very fast-growing species from New Zealand. It has large oval to round leaves about 11 cm long by 7 cm broad, markedly yellowish green in colour. Evergreen; flowers from June to September.

Blackberry, Bramble
Rubus fruticosus
Dris

Blackberry, Bramble

Blackberries are deciduous or semi-evergreen shrubs with prickly and woody scrambling stems. New shoots are produced from the base each year which lengthen and strengthen during their first year, then flower, fruit and die in their second year. After that the dead branches provide a useful skeleton through which the next year's shoots can grow, creating a dense and often impenetrable jungle. Like the shoots, blackberry leaves are prickly and are divided into three to five leaflets, very variable in shape and size. Their flowers are 20 to 30 mm broad, white or pink. The familiar fruits, made up of lots of separate fleshy segments each containing a single seed, change from green to red and finally ripen to purplish black.

A native, blackberry bushes occur abundantly in Ireland. They have the ability to produce seeds without having to be pollinated and so each bush is genetically isolated and any chance change in the genes can give rise to a new micro-species. Over 2,000 such micro-species have been named and described, making the group a nightmare for botanists. Deciduous/semi-evergreen; flowers from June to August.

Wild Cherry
Prunus avium
Crann silíní fiáin

Wild Cherry

This attractive tree up to about 25 metres (80 feet) has smooth reddish brown peeling bark when mature. Younger plants have greyer bark. It produces some suckers from the base but less freely than do many other wild Irish cherries. Its leaves are oblong or oval with a toothed edge and a longish point, light dull green and hairless on top and sparsely hairy below, about 12 cm long and 5 cm broad. When young, the leaves are often slightly drooping at their tips. In autumn they can turn a rich red before dropping. Its flowers are white, usually shallowly cup-shaped and about 20 mm across, in small clusters on long slender stalks 1.5 to 4.5 cm long. Its fruits are round, about 1 cm in diameter, dark red, and normally bitter to taste.

The wild cherry is widespread in Ireland, mainly in old hedges and woodlands. Elsewhere it occurs throughout Europe, North Africa and western Asia. Cherry wood was much used for cabinet-making, musical instruments and smoking pipes, as it is hard and dark reddish brown, similar to some tropical hardwoods such as mahogany. Wild cherries can be used in cooking but tend to have less flesh per fruit than their cultivated cousins and need more sugar. It is usually necessary to pick them before they are completely ripe as they are quickly cleared by the birds. They can also be used for cherry brandy or wine. Deciduous; flowers from April to May.

Wild Plum
Prunus domestica
Baláiste

Wild Plum

The wild plum is a large tree or shrub up to 12 metres (40 feet) tall rather similar to *P. spinosa*, the blackthorn, but with brown bark and less spiny branches. Its leaves are 3 to 8 cm long, oval or somewhat elongated and, unlike the previous species, rather hairy. It has large white flowers which appear at about the same time as the leaves. *P. domestica* is an introduced species and is well distributed in the wild in Ireland, especially in the east and the midlands. The greengage and damson are cultivated varieties *(subsp. insititia)* derived from the wild plum. Wild plums are larger than sloes and are certainly better to eat but they are still rather bitter. They become sweeter after they have suffered a few frosts and can then be used in cooking or for wine.

Several hundred cultivated varieties of the plum are grown in gardens and orchards *(subsp. domestica)* and have larger fruit which can be yellow, red, purple, green or blue-black in colour. Deciduous; flowers from April to May.

Dwarf Cherry • Prunus cerasus • *Crann sílíní searbha*

This species usually grows as a densely suckering shrub, but as a tree can reach a height of up to about 8 metres (25 feet). It is similar to *P. avium*, differing principally by having saucer-shaped flowers in smaller clusters of usually two to four, on shorter stalks than those of the previous species. Its leaves are also hairless and do not droop at their tips when young. Its fruits are bright red and always bitter to taste.

Garden, sour and morello cherries are all varieties of *P. cerasus* and many wild Irish trees are probably derived from these, sown in the wild by birds. The dwarf cherry is widely distributed in Ireland, mainly in hedges. It is frequent in some areas but in others quite rare. Its original wild origins are somewhat uncertain but it probably came from south-western Asia, perhaps arising as a hybrid cross between the wild cherry and another European or Asian species. Deciduous; flowers from April to May.

Bird Cherry • Prunus padus • *Donnroisc*

This is a shrub or tree up to about 15 metres (50 feet) tall but usually rather less, whose brown peeling bark has a strong unpleasant smell. Its leaves are 60 to 100 mm long, from oval to lanceolate in shape and with finely toothed edges, and are hairless or with white hair tufts along the leaf midrib underneath. The arrangement of the flowers in long, usually hanging or drooping heads (called racemes) makes this species easy to recognise. Flowers are 15 mm across, white and with a scent of almonds. Fruits are small, 6 to 8 mm, almost round and shiny black in colour.

The native bird cherry is quite rare in Ireland although widely distributed. It is located frequently in parts of the north-west, growing in woods and thickets, especially on damp soils in rocky places. Outside Ireland it occurs throughout Europe and is found across Asia to the Himalayas. It is widely planted for ornament and a number of cultivated forms are grown, one with semi-double flowers and another with purple leaves and pale pink flowers. Deciduous; flowers from May to June.

Portuguese Laurel
Prunus lusitanica
Labhras portaingéalach

Portuguese Laurel

This can be a tree up to 17 metres (55 feet), but is more commonly a bushy shrub up to 6 metres (20 feet), with dark green, hairless, glossy leaves, about 5 cm broad and 12 cm long, oval in shape with toothed edges and short points and short reddish stalks. Its flowers are in long heads (called racemes) 10 to 25 cm long, scattered along the shoots or occasionally at their ends. Flowers are white and about 1 cm across. The fruits are very dark purple and about 8 mm in length.

It is commonly planted in woods, especially in old demesnes, and in shrubberies. Portuguese laurel is native to Spain, Portugal and the islands of the Canaries, Madeira and the Azores where it forms interesting and ancient laurel woods. Evergreen; flowers from May to June.

Cherry Laurel
Prunus laurocerasus
Labhras silíní

Cherry Laurel

This is a large and spreading fast-growing shrub or small tree up to 7 metres (23 feet). Its leaves are oblong, up to 20 cm long, dark green and glossy, pointed but with a hardly toothed edge. When bruised, the leaves have a bitter almond fragrance, derived from a chemical close to cyanide. Indeed, the leaves are deadly poisonous. The white flowers are borne in upright heads (called racemes) like the previous species but are smaller, about 8 mm across. Fruits are similar to those of *P. lusitanica*, small, turning from red to dark purple.

The cherry laurel is very commonly planted in gardens, woods, estate woodlands and shrubberies. It quite frequently self-seeds and grows wild in many parts, especially in the southern half of Ireland. Although it is native to eastern Europe and Asia Minor it has been widely cultivated in gardens in the British Isles for several centuries. Evergreen; flowers from April to June.

Crab Apple
MAlus sylvestris
Crann fia-úll

Crab Apple

This small tree or large shrub up to 10 metres (32 feet) tall has a grey-brown scaly and fissured bark when mature and reddish brown twigs that are often spiny. Its leaves are oval and toothed, hairless when mature and up to 4 cm long. Its flowers are pink and white, 2 to 3 cm across. Its fruits are the familiar crab apples, yellowish green, sometimes flushed with red, only 2 or 3 cm broad and looking like typical but miniature apples.

The native crab apple is widely distributed in Ireland, in hedges, woodlands and scrub, and is quite common in many districts. It occurs throughout Europe and reaches into south-western Asia. Its fruits are best in September or October and are used not raw as they are very bitter, but for making jelly (crab apple jelly sets quickly and easily), wine, cider and for a vinegar called verjuice that is used as one would lemon juice. Crab apple wood is good for carving, having a very even texture and an attractive rosy brown colour. It was formerly used for making printing blocks and the heads of golf clubs.

The cultivated apple is *Malus domestica*. It can be distinguished from the crab apple by its persistently hairy leaves and its flower stalks (pedicles) covered with woolly hairs. Although not native to Ireland, it is quite widely established in the wild, mainly in and around larger towns and cities, growing from pips in discarded apple cores. Deciduous; flowers in May.

Rowan, Mountain Ash
Sorbus aucuparia
Caorthann

Rowan, Mountain Ash

Also called quicken tree, this is a slim and attractive tree with smooth grey bark, up to 20 metres (65 feet) but usually less. Its leaves are divided into about fifteen longish narrow leaflets with sharply toothed edges. Each leaflet is about 5 cm long and altogether a leaf is about 15 cm in length. The white or cream flowers are numerous and about 8 mm across and produced in dense heads. The clustered spherical fruits are scarlet, about 1 cm across, containing several seeds in the orange flesh.

A native of Ireland, the mountain ash is quite common throughout the country, growing in light soil by mountain streams and valleys, in woods and many rocky habitats. Although it grows at higher altitudes than any other Irish tree it is also a common ornamental tree in gardens and for street planting and occurs as a diverse range of cultivated varieties with variously coloured fruits and leaves. It is also found throughout Europe and into Asia Minor.

The rowan is widely featured in old Irish legends and traditions, and was an important tree in pre-Christian times, being held sacred by the Druids. It was supposed to have magic and protective qualities and was used as a talisman against evil and witchcraft. The rowan was used to prevent fires from being bewitched on May 1st, and on the same day a branch would be tied to the churn to prevent the milk from being stolen.

Its fruits, mixed with crab apples, are useful for wine and jelly. Rowan jelly is excellent with many meats. Deciduous; flowers from May to June.

Irish Whitebeam
Sorbus hibernica
Bíoma bán

Irish Whitebeam

The Irish whitebeam is a shrub or small tree up to about 6 metres (20 feet) high. It is found only in Ireland and is widely distributed in the west, midlands and east of the country, but rare in the north and south. It has oval, undivided leaves, very regularly toothed except at their base. It is hairless above and covered with white hairs underneath when the leaves first open. The hairs gradually turn to pale grey as the leaf matures. Its flowers are 12 to 15 mm across in dense heads and are followed in autumn by red fruits.

The Irish whitebeam is an attractive tree found in woods, hedges, rocky places and scrubs on limestone soils. Its berries are edible and best to use when they start to soften after several late autumn frosts. Deciduous; flowers from May to June.

Several other native whitebeams are found, each one broadly similar to the Irish whitebeam and rather difficult to distinguish from it. However, *Sorbus aria* is most widespread in County Galway and has a more markedly white underside to its leaves. *Sorbus rupicola* has leaf edges which are not toothed in their lowest third; it is rather rarely seen, only in the west and north. *Sorbus devoniensis*, a species with orange-brown fruits, is found only in the south-east and *Sorbus anglica*, a red-fruited species with rather divided leaves, is known only from around Killarney.

Cotoneaster
Contoneaster integrifolius (C.microphyllus)
Cotóinéastar mionduilleach

Cotoneaster

A range of cotoneaster species is commonly grown in Ireland in gardens. They are native to much of Europe, except Ireland, as well as northern Asia and North Africa. All are shrubs with small, waxy, mostly evergreen leaves. One of the commonest that escapes into the wild is *C. integrifolius*, an Asian species, more generally known as *C. microphyllus*. It is a small shrub with prostrate or ascending branches up to 1 metre (3 feet) long. Its small, oblong, shiny evergreen leaves are 5 to 9 mm long. Its white flowers occur singly and are 8 to 10 mm across with five petals. The fruits are red and globular, 5 to 8 mm across.

This cotoneaster is widely distributed in Ireland, especially in the west, having become established mainly in rocky or gravelly habitats from bird-distributed seeds. Another species that is also seen both in gardens and the wild in Ireland is *C. horizontalis*, from China. It is deciduous and a more robust shrub with generally larger leaves and a characteristic herring-bone arrangement to its branches. Its flowers are in ones or twos but are otherwise similar to *C. integrifolius*. Evergreen; flowers from May to June.

Broom
Cytisus scoparius
Giolcach sléibhe

Broom

The broom grows as a shrub up to about 2 metres (6.5 feet) tall, has large, bright, lemon-yellow pea-like flowers and green branchlets. Its leaves are divided into three oval leaflets and arranged alternately on the five-angled shoots. However, the leaves are soon lost as the branchlets mature. Its flowers are about 2 cm long and its seed capsules are black, with brown hairs along the edges, and 2.5 to 4 cm in length.

Native to Ireland, it occurs in dry heathy places, open woods, on dry banks and roadsides and is widespread throughout the country but rarely common. It occurs through Europe, growing on light lime-free soils only. The broom obtained its name from the former use of its branches for making brushes. A rare prostrate form with silky leaves is found on a few coastal cliffs and is worth looking out for. A wide range of European species and cultivated varieties are grown in Irish gardens. Evergreen; flowers from May to June.

Gorse, Furze or Whin
Ulex europaeus
Aiteann gallda

Gorse, Furze or Whin

When gorse is in flower, kissing is in fashion – so goes the old expression. The two species of gorse in Ireland flower at different times, one in spring, *U. europaeus*, and the other, *U. gallii*, in autumn, so there is rarely a week of the year when some flowers cannot be found.

The native *U. europaeus* is a very spiny and bushy shrub with blue-green branchlets and leaves reduced to small scales or thorns. It can grow to more than 2 metres (6.5 feet) tall. It is found throughout Ireland, especially in the east on lime-free soils in rough pastures, heaths and rocky places, but not in woodlands. In the west and on higher mountain slopes it is replaced by the next species. In some areas it was planted to form hedges.

Gorse was formerly used for fuel and was a good fodder source for stock once its spines had been crushed, usually with large stone rollers or wooden mallets. Gorse flower wine is, I am told, worth trying. Its flowers are golden yellow, sweetly scented and from 15 to 20 mm long, surrounded by a short hairy brown calyx. The seeds develop in a small pea–pod-like black capsule that when mature is similar in length to the flowers. During dry summer days one can often hear the cracking open of pods as they explode to disperse the seeds. It is widespread throughout western Europe and North Africa and introduced to many other parts of the world.

Ulex europaeus "strictus", a variety with erect branches and soft, flexible spines, was first discovered as a once-off chance freak plant in Northern Ireland in the 19th century. It is now a frequently grown garden plant. Evergreen; flowers from April to June.

Mountain Gorse, Western Gorse
Ulex gallii
Aiteann gaelach

Mountain Gorse, Western Gorse

The native mountain gorse is also a bushy shrub but is a smaller, darker green species than the previous one, less hairy and with smaller, deeper yellow flowers. It can also be distinguished by having only faintly furrowed spines whereas those of *U. europaeus* are deeply furrowed. Its seed pods are burst open in spring. It occurs distributed along the Atlantic coastal fringes of Europe, from Spain to Scotland. Evergreen; flowers from August to October.

Fuchsia
Fuchsia magellanica
Fiúise

Fuchsia

Many people find it hard to believe that fuchsia is not a native plant in Ireland. It comes from Chile and Argentina but has long been used here in gardens and as a hedge plant. It is easy to grow from cuttings, tolerates strong winds and will grow well even in quite boggy or peaty soils, making it ideal for western Ireland.

Fuchsia forms a bushy and spreading shrub up to 3 metres (10 feet) tall, but never a tree. Its bark is a light yellowish brown and peeling. Its leaves are opposite, oval and toothed, about 2.5 to 6 cm long, with short stalks. Its distinctive drooping flowers are produced singly along the stems and consist of four bright red sepals arising from the end of a swollen tube and four deep purple petals from which protrude the eight long stamens. In autumn the fruits are black, fleshy, almost spherical berries 1.5 to 2 cm long.

The commonest variety found is *var. riccartonii*, which originally arose as a garden variety. It has fat spherical buds which pop when squeezed. A rarer variety, *magellanica proper*, has longer and thinner buds. Fuchsia does not tolerate too much frost and so is rarest in the midlands, east and north. Deciduous; flowers from July to September.

Dogwood
Cornus sanguinea
Conbhaiscne

Dogwood

C. sanguinea grows to be a shrub up to 4 metres (13 feet) tall but is usually somewhat smaller. Its leaves are rather unpleasant smelling, arranged opposite each other on the shoots, oval to elliptical in shape, 4 to 10 cm long, covered on top and underneath with short, flattened, soft hairs. The leaves turn purple-red in autumn before they are dropped and new shoots also turn dark red then. Dogwood flowers are whitish with four petals, clustered together in dense, more or less flat-topped, heads. The fruits are dark purple to black and berry-like, 5 to 8 mm across.

The dogwood is rather rare in Ireland as a native and confined to limestone soils in woods, scrub and rocky places mainly in the midlands. It also occurs occasionally as a garden escape. Its fruits can be made into jam and have been used to flavour liqueurs in parts of Europe.

A closely related but non-native species, *C. sericea*, the red osier dogwood from eastern North America, is established quite widely in Ireland often on water margins, as an escape from gardens, parks and demesnes. It is also a deciduous shrub but spreads freely by numerous suckering shoots. It has white or creamy coloured flowers which are smaller than those of *C. sanguinea*. Deciduous; flowers from June to July.

Spindle-tree
Euonymus europaeus
Feoras

Spindle-tree

Worldwide there are over 175 species of *Euonymus*, widely distributed across Europe and Asia, most of them shrubs. The ubiquitous and dull, variegated evergreen shrub, *E. japonicus*, is well known and all too commonly grown as a hedging plant.

The only wild Irish spindle-tree is a small easily overlooked deciduous shrubby tree with smooth grey bark and shortly stalked, opposite, oval to lanceolate leaves, slightly toothed on their edges, and four-angled green twigs. The latter characteristic is the easiest way of identifying the species, winter or summer. It is an unremarkable species except when in fruit. The fruits are orange-red in colour and surrounded by a rose-pink fleshy sheath called an aril. In autumn, a spindle-tree well laden with fruits can be a most striking sight. Its flowers are small, inconspicuous and greenish, occuring in the axils of the leaves.

A native, *E. europaeus* is widespread, especially in the centre and parts of the west, but rarer in the east and north. It is commonest in woods, hedgerows and thickets and frequent in rocky places and lake shores, particularly on limestone soils.

Spindle-trees produce a durable white timber, formerly used for making spindles, viola bows, skewers and toothpicks. The whole plant is poisonous though. Deciduous; flowers from May to June.

Holly
ilex aquifolium
Cuileann

Holly

The native holly is a densely branched small tree or shrub that is widespread in Europe and North Africa. In Ireland, it is widespread in woodlands, especially oak woods, as an undergrowth tree and in hedges.

The slow-growing holly produces very hard and durable wood and is used for such purposes as tool handles. It makes an excellent fuel wood. As a winter decoration its use goes back in Ireland to pre-Christian times. The tree was regarded as "gentle" in Ireland and beloved of the fairies. Sprigs brought into the house were useful to ward off evil spirits which were especially wary of the scarlet fruits.

The berries are unpleasant tasting but apparently not poisonous. The leaves are alternate, hard, bright or dark green on their upper surfaces and with spiny buckled edges. The small white flowers are noticeably fragrant. Male and female flowers are produced on separate trees and so holly berries are only to be found on the females. The berries can last all winter until the following summer, unless cleared by birds, especially fieldfares in February, or if cut off by humans for Christmas. Evergreen; flowers from May to June.

Buckthorn
Rhamnus catharticus
Paide bréan

Buckthorn

The native buckthorn is not a common plant in Ireland although in a few areas, particularly in the north and west, it is locally common. It grows on limestone soils as a shrub or small tree 4 to 6 metres (13 to 20 feet) tall, occurring in woods, scrub, river banks and rocky lake shores. It is a rather unremarkable tree without any easily recognisable features. Its branches are often rather spiny and arise in opposite pairs almost at right angles to the main stem. Its leaves are usually alternate, undivided, 3 to 6 mm long, oval or slightly elongated with a toothed edge. Its flowers are very small with four green petals. The fruits are black, berry-like and inedible. Deciduous; flowers from May to June.

A close relation, *Frangula alnus*, the alder buckthorn (*Draighean fearna*), is a much rarer native deciduous small tree or shrub of rocky or boggy habitats. Although it has been recorded in about half the Irish counties, it is nowhere common. It is similar in leaf to the buckthorn but it has five petals, is not spiny and its fruits are red, gradually turning black.

Horse Chestnut
Aesculus hippocastanum
Crann cnó capaill

Horse Chestnut

It is ironic that one of the most familiar Irish trees is not a native tree and indeed is rare and even endangered in the wild. The horse chestnut is native to parts of the Balkans, found in Greece, Albania and in a single site in Bulgaria. It has been grown in Ireland as an ornamental tree for over 200 years and although it is still commonly planted it has self-seeded and spread into wild habitats in woods and hedges throughout Ireland.

The horse chestnut grows to be a magnificent, large, spreading tree with broad leaves divided into five to seven leaflets. Its bark varies in colour from reddish brown to dark grey-brown. Its twigs and branches are robust and in winter bear large, sticky brown buds. In spring the tree produces large upright branched heads (panicles) of white flowers with five petals speckled with pink or yellow spots. In September the globular and spiny fruit capsules are produced containing one or two dark brown (chestnut-coloured!) fruits or "conkers".

The tree is little used except as an ornamental and for its conkers. Its timber is soft and pithy. The common name is said to be derived from the former use of its fruits having been ground up for horse feed, although as they contain copious amounts of the chemical saponin (a useful soap substitute) they cannot be very tasty, even for horses. Deciduous; flowers in May.

Sycamore
Acer pseudoplatanus
Seiceamar

Sycamore

Although the sycamore is one of the most familiar Irish trees, it is not native, having been introduced to the British Isles in the 15th or 16th century. It grows to be a large and occasionally a magnificent tree with greyish bark. More often it is a small weedy tree of waste places, woods, hedges and gardens. Although native to the European mountains, it is completely happy in the Irish climate and indeed makes an excellent shelter-belt tree for coastal situations.

Sycamore produces a valuable pale creamy coloured wood. Sycamore wood table-tops maintain a smooth white surface despite constant scrubbing; it was also used for rolling pins, wooden spoons, the sides and backs of violins and is also a popular wood for carving.

The leaves are typically maple-shaped, 9 to 12 cm across, with five pointed lobes and a coarsely toothed edge. The flowers are small and greenish and occur in drooping heads; they are a useful source of early spring nectar for honey bees. The seeds are always popular with children as mini "helicopters", having two divergent membranous wings on each side of the two-jointed fruit.

A close relative, *A. campestre*, the field maple, also an introduction, is occasionally planted in hedges in the east. It has much smaller leaves. Deciduous; flowers from May to June.

Ivy
Hedera helix
Eidhneán

Ivy

Although not strictly a tree or shrub, this native climber is included because it can become very woody, with stems up to 25 cm (10 inches) in diameter and sometimes climbing to more than 30 metres (100 feet) in height. It is unusual in that it produces its flowers in autumn, when they are often hungrily visited for their nectar by flies and wasps as the only flowers left at that time.

The stems of ivy are densely covered with clinging roots. The small flowers in rounded heads have five yellow-green petals, 3 to 4 mm long, and are followed by round black berries 6 to 8 mm in size. Ivy leaves are a glossy dark green, hairless and easily recognised by their characteristic five lobes, spread out somewhat like the fingers of a hand. The leaves of flowering branches are without lobes and more oval in shape. Ivy only flowers in the sun towards the top of whatever it is climbing on.

Ivy is common in woodlands, hedgerows, rocks, walls or creeping along the ground in shady woods or hedgebanks. Evergreen; flowers from October to November.

Butterfly Bush
Buddleia davidii
Tor an fhéileacáin

Butterfly Bush

This large shrub is a relative newcomer to Ireland. It is native to China where it was discovered by Augustine Henry, a famous Irish plants and forestry pioneer who first collected many important Chinese plants. Until the middle of this century buddleia was grown only in gardens, but over the last few decades it began an explosive invasion of many urban habitats throughout the country. Now it is one of the commonest weeds of Ireland's larger towns and cities, especially Dublin. Spreading easily by seed, it is an important food plant for butterflies which are attracted to the nectar-rich flowers.

B. davidii grows up to 4 metres (13 feet) tall and has long (10 to 20 cm) lanceolate leaves, green on top, white and felty underneath. The flowers are lilac-mauve, small and tubular with an orange eye, borne in massed conical heads. Fruits are small, dry, brown capsules.

Several different attractive colour varieties of *B. davidii* are grown in gardens, from white to purple, as well as some other related species. Deciduous; flowers from June to September.

Ash
Fraxinus excelsior
Fuinseóg

Ash

A tall native tree up to 40 metres (130 feet) with grey bark, smooth when young but becoming grooved with interwoven fissures when older. Ash twigs are thick and grey with large conspicuous black buds in winter. The leaves are opposite and divided into nine to fifteen jaggedly toothed, long (about 7 cm), narrow leaflets. The flowers are tiny, purple and without petals or sepals and appear in dense clusters well before the leaves in spring. Male and female flowers often occur on separate branches. The fruits (called keys) are long and slim, 25 to 50 mm long, with a single membranous wing, ideal to catch the wind for easy distribution. They are produced in dense dangling clusters.

Ash is a common and often abundant tree of the Irish countryside, in woods and hedges. It grows best on deep, moist, lime-rich soils but is not very fussy about its habitat. It provides one of the most important native timbers, pale brown in colour, lightweight and flexible but very tough. It has been used for carts, furniture, ladders, table-tops and a range of sports implements such as tennis rackets and hurley sticks ("the clash of the ash") as it is fine grained and smooth to the hand. Ash wood is also good for fuel and even burns well when fresh and green. It is an altogether useful species and even its fruits can be eaten, if picked very young, boiled and pickled in vinegar. Deciduous; flowers from April to May.

Wild Privet
Ligustrum vulgare
Pribhéad

Wild Privet

This is a semi-evergreen shrub that can grow up to about 4 metres (13 feet) tall, with young shoots that are densely covered by short hairs. It has opposite, shortly stalked, untoothed leaves, oblong to lanceolate in shape, pointed at their ends and 3 to 6 cm long. Its flowers are white, 4 to 5 mm in diameter with a long tube. The flowers are followed by shining black fruits 6 to 8 mm long. Wild privet is very rare in Ireland and only occurs naturally on a few cliffs and rocky habitats in four counties, as well as throughout Europe and North Africa. However, in Ireland it is also widespread as a planted species in hedges and gardens, mainly grown from cuttings. Its seeds germinate very slowly.

It could be easily confused with a closely related species, *L. ovalifolium*, the Japanese or garden privet, which is now more widely planted for hedges than its wild relative. Japanese privet can be distinguished by being more reliably evergreen, with broader leaves and hairless shoots. Variegated or yellow-leaved colour variants of the Japanese privet are also widely cultivated but are rather less strong-growing than the typical form. Semi-evergreen; flowers from June to July.

Elder
Sambucus nigra
Trom

Elder

The elder is a tree or shrub up to 10 metres (33 feet) tall. It is easily recognisable by its grey to light brown corky and grooved bark. Second-year shoots are covered by numerous raised spots called lenticels. It often produces new shoots straight from the base which is just as well as it is a rather brittle tree whose branches collapse quite frequently. Its leaves are opposite and divided into five to nine leaflets resembling those of an ash. Each leaflet is 5 to 15 cm long and has a strong unpleasant smell. Its flowers are white and fragrant, very small and with five petals. They occur in dense flat-topped heads 10 to 25 cm across; they have pale yellow anthers. The fruits are black and berry-like when ripe and contain three seeds each. They are very juicy and succulent and full of dark red flesh that is ideal for wine making. When the soft pith is removed from the centre of young shoots, these can be cut and grooved to make quite satisfactory home-made flutes.

It was a custom in rural Ireland to scoop up clay from under an elder bush to soothe an aching tooth. Both the flowers and the fruit are used to make drinks; the flowers make a refreshing summer soft drink and the fruit a traditional wine. The fruit must not be muddled up with the very similar berries of the much smaller Danewort (*Sambucus ebulus*) which are poisonous.

The elder is native in Ireland but also widely planted. It is often associated with disturbed soils and is a frequent tree of waste grounds in town and cities, preferring soils rich in nitrogen that often accompany human settlements. It also occurs commonly in woods and hedges. Deciduous; flowers from June to July.

Guelder-rose
Viburnum opulus
Caoir chon

CAPRIFOLIACEAE – THE ELDER FAMILY

Guelder-Rose

Guelder-rose is a deciduous shrub 2 to 4 metres (6 to 13 feet) tall that is widespread in Europe, Asia and just reaches North Africa. A native of Ireland, it occurs in woods, scrub and hedges and is frequent, particularly on moist soils.

Its leaves are 4 to 8 cm long with three or five pointed lobes and an irregularly toothed edge, turning reddish in autumn. It produces flat rather loose heads of white flowers some 5 to 10 cm across. The outer flowers are sterile, 15 to 20 mm across with large showy petals, there only to attract insects for pollination. The inner flowers are fertile and about half the size. Geoffrey Grigson in *The Englishman's Flora* suggests that the flowers have a fragrance of "crisply fried well-peppered trout" which is something I will take his word for. In autumn the flowers are followed by crimson berries that are not very popular with birds as they contain lots of bitter valerianic acid but can be used to make a tasty and tangy jelly if you add lots of sugar.

The snowball tree is a well-known garden plant that is a variant of this species. It only has sterile flowers which are clustered together in a globular head. Another close relative, *V. lanata*, the wayfaring tree, is an introduction and is occasionally planted in hedges in the east. It can be distinguished by its oval leaves and flower heads which only have fertile flowers. Deciduous; flowers from June to July.

Snowberry
Symphoricarpos albus
Póirín sneachta

Snowberry

This is a small, twiggy shrub widely planted in hedges and thence spreading by suckers, rarely by seed. It is a useful garden plant which thrives in shade and will tolerate very low temperatures and frost. It is native to North America.

Snowberry has small oval leaves and pinky white small tubular flowers in terminal heads. Its fruits are globular, 1 to 1.5 cm across, white marble-like and very conspicuous in winter especially when the leaves have dropped. The fruits are variously described as "edible" to "poisonous" in different reference books, so I would not chance eating them myself! Deciduous; flowers from June to September.

GLOSSARY

Alternate/opposite leaves: the arrangement of leaves on a stem is a useful characteristic to help identify many plants. They may be produced opposite each or staggered alternately.

Anther: small, usually stalked, sacks of pollen; the male parts of a flower.

Bract: modified leaves found between the calyx and the true leaves.

Calyx: a collective name for the sepals which occur next to the petals but are generally more leaf-like.

Catkin: lamb's-tail-like structures in which plants bear their flowers. They usually hang down into the wind to disperse or catch pollen.

Coppice: some trees and shrubs will produce a mass of new growth when their branches are cut down to ground level, or nearly so. This process, called coppicing, is often carried out as part of a regular maintenance routine to produce long straight sticks and posts (see *pollard).*

Hybrid: a cross between individuals of different species.

Lanceolate: long and narrow like a lance.

Leaflet: some leaves are subdivided into separate portions called leaflets.

Needle: conifer leaves that are usually long and very narrow.

Pollard: some trees will produce a mass of new growth when their upper branches are heavily pruned. This is often carried out as part of a regular maintenance routine and is called pollarding (see *coppice).*

Pollen: small single cells produced by male organs in the flowers, containing genetic material, which is used to pollinate the female flowers.

Sepal: (see *calyx).*

Species: a group of closely related individuals with common characteristics which are able to interbreed freely with each other.

Subspecies: a sub-division within a species linking closely related individuals that share a number of common characteristics which differ from other members of their own species.

Stigmas: the female part of the flower on which pollen lands for fertilisation.

Stipule: leaf-like wings produced at the bases of the leaf-stalks of some trees and shrubs.

Suckers: new shoots produced from the base or underground roots of an established plant.

BIBLIOGRAPHY

Bean, W. J., *Trees and Shrubs Hardy in the British Isles,* 8th edition (London: John Murray, 1970–1988). *Exhaustive work on British and Irish trees and shrubs, wild and cultivated.*

Clapham, A. R., Tutin, T. G. and Moore, D. M., *Flora of the British Isles,* 3rd edition (Cambridge: Cambridge University Press, 1987). *A very comprehensive guide.*

Meikle, R. D., *Willows and Poplars of Great Britain and Ireland* (London: Botanical Society of the British Isles, 1984). *A specialist's guide to a difficult group of trees and shrubs.*

Mitchell, A., *A Field Guide to the Trees of Britain and Northern Europe* (London: Collins, 1974). *Still the best available comprehensive compact guide to trees of Britain and Ireland, with good illustrations.*

Mitchell, F., *Shell Guide to Reading the Irish Landscape* (Dublin: Country House, 1986). *A fascinating book on the origins of Ireland's flora and landscape.*

Phillips, R., *Trees in Britain, Europe and North America* (London: Pan Books, 1978). *A photographic guide to more than 500 trees.*

Phillips, R., *Wild Food* (London: Pan Books, 1983). *An excellent guide to collecting, cooking and eating wild plants, containing dozens of good photographs and recipes.*

Scannell, M. J. P. and Synnott, D. M., *Census Catalogue of the Flora of Ireland,* 2nd edition (Dublin: Stationery Office, 1987). *Plots the distribution of Ireland's flora on a county by county basis and includes all their Latin, English and Irish names.*

Stace, C., *New Flora of the British Isles* (Cambridge: Cambridge University Press, 1992). *The newest and most up-to-date Flora of Britain and Ireland.*

Tutin, T. G. and others, *Flora Europaea* (Cambridge: Cambridge University Press, 1964–1980). *A full guide to Europe's plants in 5 volumes. Volume 1 has recently been revised and republished in 1993.*

Webb, D. A., *An Irish Flora,* 6th edition (Dundalk: Dundalgan Press, 1977). *The definitive field guide to all of Ireland's wild plants.*